I'M

F.I.N.E.

FUCKED-UP, INSECURE, NEUROTIC, AND EMOTIONAL

NICHOL RONÉE BOURDEAUX

For the wolves that raised me

Contents

A STRANGE BEAUTIFUL WOMAN

A strange beautiful woman
met me in the mirror
the other night.
Hey,
I said,
What you doing here?
She asked me
the same thing.

— *Marilyn Nelson*

I'M

F.I.N.E.

FUCKED-UP, INSECURE, NEUROTIC, AND EMOTIONAL

fucked-up

Adjective \ ˈfəkt-ˈəp \

Definition of fucked-up
vulgar slang: damaged,
obscene, misguided, and
broken

PHANTOM LOVE

Imprint in my bed
in my heart
Relationship scar-tissue remains.

Prayers to God to fill both with grace and love
Prayers answered?
Why now, why?

God's exhale propels us out of gravity
No matter
No light
Our touch, our thrusts.

Minutes, hours,
days, elapse
We move together.

Our love, your love
Escaping the pull is fruitless
Shadowed imprint of your soul remains.

The kaleidoscope erupts
With one inhale
Love lands at God's feet.

PERFECTION

drawn by anticipated rejection
or compulsion for love
fate pulls me to you

begging you to see me
as you see color
vivid, playful, beloved
to be used

your subject made real, me
the art you choose to master
meticulously sculpted shapes
tedious strokes of color
illuminated by light
masked by shadows

use me to obtain perfection
your art to be valued, revered
the feat of time
precision not all can achieve

and, let my desperation and ignorance
hide on the dark side of the folds
sheltered by your love

MANCHILD GRASPING HIS ROPE

Things have always come easy to you
the smile, the charm, the money

no harm from life's misfortunes
afflictions only promise charity
and fear stays at bay.

What happens when the charm fails
harm begins
and the world ends?

No mommy, no daddy
to certify your mind
their shrinking approval
leaves no path to fame.

Only insanity remains
on the veiled face of your constraint.

BORDERLINES

I see you
perfecting the art of the eye
while destroying the strength of the heart
ignoring remnants of meals
curated in health and hate
your day-to-day chores pushed aside
thoughtless priorities of the mediocre

Your mind and body take comfort
under blankets of security
the mind locked into a snug fog
of reaffirming thoughts

With each day a promise declared
to prove your sanity
brush strokes give distinction
following meticulous borders of color

A perimeter
perfected realism in keen hues
giving fictious depth
to the two dimensional

the borders remain
constraining and securing
on the canvas and in your mind
your straitjacket is at arm's length

Cry now, smile later
keep those who know
under the restraints of your smile
they remain on the backside of your borders

OH, LOVE

I sit with my body contorted looking to get warmth from my own arms, eyes swollen, hands shaking, the hint of your smell bringing comfort. The last time I saw you I was different, strong in my conviction. My body positioned for attack, ready to head off your charm. This time my hands are shaking, my bowels growling from days of pills for sustenance. I can't stop the tears no matter how hard I try. I am lost in knowing that I am the victim of my decision. Strong before and determined to end it, now all I want is for the pain of my decision to cease. You look strong in your discernment, determined to move away from this teeter-totter of emotion. Leaning into me, proving there are no more questions, your lips part as you flash me that tender smile and gently kiss me on the forehead.

He said, "Love is pain."
I need love to be easy.
Oh, love, no more love.

LIGHTNING IN A BOTTLE

As she walks away
he flicks the bottle back into the water

The bottle is drawn from the shore
tumbled and submerged by foam
(she doesn't look back)

He continues to stroll the beach dismissing the bottle
as one would a cigarette butt in a dirty ashtray

It will take him a lifetime to learn
what she knows from a life of beach combing

insecure

Adjective \ in-si-'kyur \

Definition of insecure:
erratic, weak, and encompassed
by anxiety and fear.

BLACK DEBRIS

The remnants of your departure: black circles in my mind and on my face. Hidden by compound shades of laughter black circles with no resolve surrounding eyes of emptiness.

Orbital thoughts of ceaseless loneliness reflect the face in the mirror. Concentric emotion of the soul and mind tornado the debris of nothingness: black circles.

THE END OF THE 2OTH CENTURY

I believe in the inherent good of the soul
you say "everyone is selfish"

      I cannot hear

My mind is filled with endless rainbows,
life is never-ending

      I cannot see

My world consists of realists
the world will bend to our will

      I cannot know

We pick dandelions full of possibility,
expelling a full breath of expectancy

      I cannot breathe

Anticipated dreams of utopian cities,
lovers and unconditional love

      I cannot feel

More and more we await a new vision, one of us,
to lead us out of the murderous pain of day-to-day
Imagination, tenacity, ambition

I cannot follow
you

HIDING UNDER MY DESK

Trouble, don't trouble me
I don't trouble you.
Trouble those who trouble you
The ones with no empathy, no trust, just self.

Trouble, don't trouble me
I don't trouble you.
For my bank is far too empty from years of pain and plight.
Trouble those with just arrogance
and who laugh at life's strife.

Trouble, don't trouble me
I don't trouble, you.
For I know that an empty soul has no trouble to give.

So, trouble those who ignore the pain of others
with no regard and no fight, they just live.
And for me, I will not trouble Trouble
until Trouble troubles me.

NO ONE MAKES THE GRADE

He loved, love, loves me.
I test, test, test, test his love.
They all fail the test.

BLACK ELLIPSIS

"...

I meant...

Um, no not that...

Oh, sorry, yes...

I mean...no.

So, when I say this, I don't mean that.

Oh, did I interrupt you?

Oh, did I mumble?

Sorry.

No...I am sorry.

Angry...No, confused.

Different...Oh, please.

It's pillow...not pelllll - ow.

Ask, me...

I didn't say ax!

Yes...What he said.

No...What she said.

That's what I said.

Is that clear?

…too passionate?

…too emotional?

Too direct.

Articulate…Professional…

Well, yes…I heard you.

Can you hear me?

GRANDMA'S GHOST IN THE WALLS

Are   you   still   here?

Protecting me in the night
holding me as you did in your arms
breathing your dream of love, adventure
freedom into my soul.

Are   you   still   here?

As I fall to my knees begging God
for the man of my dreams.
A warrior to save me from the hopelessness
of black chains, the world on my shoulders
as I mind the pain of my children, their children
and no one to mind me.

Are   you   still   here?

When I rock myself to sleep
praying the monotony of achievement away
pride of a beautiful child, successful career
impeccable house in the appropriate zip code
suitable car and designer dog.

Are   you   still   here?

Watching the world collapse
around your dreams.

Oh spirit, my guardian
guide me to my purpose, my dream.
Show me the way to unequivocal love.

HURTLING RAGE

Exhausted from bouncing thoughts of truth and lies, it takes hours of playing pinball in the mind to realize we will never know what is real. The moment we feel safe and secure in what can be, all is taken away by one comment of false truth. The mind continues to grasp an idealistic narrative, yet society ensures we are not lost in our fantasy.

> All liars lie to me
> Who to trust? Not even me.
> Enraged. Who sees me?

neurotic

Adjective\ nu-ˈrä-tik, nyu- \

Definition of neurotic:
unstable, distorted reality,
visceral symptoms caused by
mental and emotional
disturbances.

FEAR OR FLIGHT

smell of flight on me

       fleeing the fear of your love

              "no, wait

              come

back!"

FLOAT

snowflakes swirling
dancing like my heart and mind
oh, where will they land?

DARK DAWN

the dark dawn at hand
steam churning in the sky. Rain
negates the day.

WINTER ASPEN LIGHT

the solemn finch tweets
gentle songs of winter blues
now my soul rises.

SOUL SEARCHING

broken souls cry out
years of torture and despair
pushing
the   world   away
questioning all existence
in the present vapid space
saving their prayers for the end of days.

QUIET THE BEE

She buzzes like a bee
>be still they say

Her mind dances and twirls
>be still they say

Her mouth lashes the truth with lighting speed
>be still they say

Buzzy, busy, playful a future to nurture
>be still they say

Eager to be the queen, she aspires to be loved by all
>be still they say

How to be still without the death of her flower
>to stop her body, her mind, her mouth

He will.

Arms contoured, the weight collapsing her lungs
>be still he says

She feels the pain as he tears into her unsullied hive
>be still he says

Silence.
>no buzzing bee, no dancing mind, no voice of truth

I am still.

emotional

Adjective\ i-ˈmō-shnəl-shə-n□l \

Definition of emotional:
dominated by feelings, arousal, a
conscious reaction spurring a
physical and behavioral
response.

MIRROR OF ME

you see me

my ashy knees crusted and cracked
heart beneath armor that protects my soul

you see me

the mind's thoughts sharp behind a profane tongue
you see my pain leavened, pounded and baked into joy

you see me

fall to my knees to meet my tears
and, rise up to hold my crown
you see my anger, stretched, pulled, and twisted into love

you see me

the mirror of true friendship allows us to be
so today my friend, let it be known
i see you

ANTIQUE MEMORIES

buried nose in yellow pages
fragrance of lavender, rosewater, and mothballs
eyes closed, drawn breath
triggers images of a quilt-covered bed
books stacked in shadowed corners
that familiar smell found in any city
with a past, and reputation
i always seem to find

TOMBOY LOOKING FOR HER PLAYMATE IN
GREEN PASTURES

You remind me of him, a Cheshire cat smile on your lips and eyes, playful, childlike, just as wide, but not sinister. I wonder if He sent you to me. To be my Shepherd in this valley. A replacement for this girl who kneels to solicit love.

I miss him now more than ever. Years pass and, in his absence, grief prevails. I miss knowing his love for me, a stored-away blanket, ready to be swaddled around the chilled heart. I miss the comfort of knowing he found his love, a family that gave him permanent space and time. Giving promise to me, his sheep.

With him gone, I struggle to know if I am that wandering sheep, looking for my Shepherd who knows my inclinations to turn right when the course is dead ahead?

Perhaps after all these years of his absence, moving forward on autopilot, I no longer need the crook. The right course is clear with a gentle flash of your spirited-smile.

DRIVING UNDER THE INFLUENCE OF ANXIETY

with one small gesture
terror engulfs every breath
purge, release control

CURFEW

where were you
during the lockdown
when the black bird's wings were broken
your brothers and sisters were there
but you said "race
should not be spoken"

PITY FOR THE SUPREMACISTS

Your insecurity empowers us
with each poke our swagger grows
pride of legacy, royalty of the past
raised the land beneath your feet.

You look to dismantle us
your dread fuels our power
liberating the rage in our hearts.

Explosions of anger met
with doubled-downed discernment
qualifying your truth
not our truth.

Soul dust ingrained in the earth
bends to our will
lifting us one by one.

Generation by generation
fortifying our future
into fruitful ascendency.

hesed

Noun\ kheh-sed \

Definition of hesed: unending,
underserving, unfailing mercy,
grace, and love.

UNEARTHING HESED

a declaration of allegiance
skipping through the scrolls of faith
pressed water on scarred pages
koran, torah, bible
    Your God, my God, no God

privilege turns away from bowed-head promises
meandering through gardens, forests, and galaxies
dead ends and no cures
    Your God, my God, no God

eyes blue or black
soul-reflecting tears pleading mercy
    Your God, my God, no God

ego-suffused veins carry sin
gross persecution and inherited oppression
    Your God, my God, no God

genuflect, bow or kneel

our will be done
    My Death, your Death, all Death

ABOUT THE AUTHOR

"Your pieces are sensitive, profound, honest and beautiful." Julie Hartley, novelist, poet, creative writing teacher.

Nichol Ronée Bourdeaux is inspired by the popular singer-songwriters of the '70s. Her simple and playful poems are meant to be read aloud to experience the melodic expression and tone. She hopes her writing opens an accessible doorway that welcomes a broader audience to other women-of-color writers. Most recently, her poems have appeared in "The Rising Phoenix Review."

Nichol Bourdeaux currently lives in Salt Lake City, Utah. She holds a BA in Communications and an MPA from the University of Utah.